MY SOUL LONGS FOR YOU

30 DAILY READINGS FOR ANY TIME OF YEAR

Thirsting for God in the Psalms

WIPF & STOCK · Eugene, Oregon

Mathew Bartlett

Wipf and Stock Publishers
199 W 8th Ave, Suite 3
Eugene, OR 97401

My Soul Longs for You
By Bartlett, Mathew
Copyright©2018 Apostolos
ISBN 13: 978-1-5326-6873-9
Publication date 9/15/2018
Previously published by Apostolos, 2018

Psalm 42: My God, I Thirst for You

Day 1: *Thirsting for God is Natural—and Necessary*

As the deer pants for streams of water, so my soul pants for you, my God. (Psalm 42:1)

What a beautiful picture from nature—a deer going down to the stream to drink. Nothing could be more natural than an animal's desire to quench its thirst! It is equally as true for plants and humans as it is for the animals—water is essential for life.

In Western countries, where most people have a reliable water supply connected to their homes, we have almost lost the understanding that without water, we die. But there are still many people in the majority world who travel great distances daily to find a source of water to survive. This helps us understand that the picture in this Psalm goes much deeper than mere thirst. The psalmist clearly saw that without God, he could not survive.

God created everything in the beginning, and gives life to all living things. He breathed into Adam, who consequently became a living soul (Gen 2:7). Hence by nature, humankind cannot experience *life* without God. The tragedy of Adam's disobedience in Eden was that humanity became separated from the source of its life, as sin broke our relationship with God. Jesus Christ came to forgive our sin, restore our relationship with God and reconnect us with the source of life. Thirsting for God is as natural—and necessary—as breathing!

> **Prayer:** Lord, you created us in the beginning, and all life comes from you. We thank you for our Lord Jesus Christ, who has reconnected us with you, the source of true life. And we thank you for the desire that you have formed in our hearts, to continue to share that life with you. Our God, we thirst and long for you, and hunger to know you more. Amen.

Daily Reading Plan Day One: Genesis 1–3; Psalm 1.

Day 2: *Deepen Your Desire for God*

My soul thirsts for God, for the living God. When can I go and meet with God? (Psalm 42:2)

Jesus Christ has restored our relationship with God as Father, and it is a recurring theme of Scripture—and of our human experience—that those who reconnect with God want more of him.

Have you ever been in a relationship where you longed to be with those whom you loved, and missed their company—perhaps even pined for them—when they were absent? I have experienced this feeling for my closest friends and family, but this is also the basis of our thirst for God. Our desire for more of God is the result of our deepening love for him. It involves a desire to have a deeper relationship, a fuller sense of his presence, and the blessing of his revealing himself to us in increasing measure.

God's relationship with us is one of love, and our response is to love him in return, and that involves seeking his companionship. When God seems to hide his face from us, we pine for him and seek him even more. We are troubled when his presence seems absent for any length of time.

Our longing for a personal and meaningful encounter with God leads us ultimately to ask: "When will I come and see the face of God?" (AMP). The Bible assures us that we shall all see his face in heaven: "The throne of God and of the Lamb will be in the city, and his servants will serve him. They will see his face, and his name will be on their foreheads (Rev 21:3–4). Only when we are in this place of intimate relationship, where God's dwelling will forever be among his people, shall our thirst be fully satisfied.

> **Prayer:** Lord, we love you because you first loved us. We long for a deeper and more intimate relationship with you as our God and heavenly Father. Teach us through your Son Jesus to develop closer companionship with you, as we await the time when we shall see you face to face and dwell with you eternally. Amen.

Daily Reading Plan Day Two: Genesis 4–5; Psalm 2.

Day 3: *Longing for God in Times of Trouble*

> *My tears have been my food day and night, while people say to me all day long, "Where is your God?" These things I remember as I pour out my soul: how I used to go to the house of God under the protection of the Mighty One with shouts of joy and praise among the festive throng. (Psalm 42:3–4)*

In the parable of the sower, Jesus warned that some people would turn away from the truth because of persecution and opposition (see Matthew 13:20–21). However, he never intended this to be the effect of opposition on the believer. Rather, as we see from the above verses, whilst opposition and the derision of unbelievers brought distress and tears, it also served to accentuate the psalmist's thirst for God.

In times of difficulty, remembering past blessings encourages us to thirst for God, especially when a lack of present blessing accentuates our sense of need. The psalmist recalled the wonderful blessings he experienced when he went with the crowd to worship God in the temple during a sacred feast. Our hope to see God's action is based on our previous experience of his goodness.

We are also encouraged by the realisation that God's nature is unchanging: his love is constant (v. 8), and his help is certain (v. 5, 11). The psalmist knows that, just as he praised God in the past, so he would praise God again. So in spite of our current difficulties, even if opposition we face for Christ is enough to depress us, we can be sure that he will eventually act on our behalf.

> **Prayer:** Lord, we feel grieved and upset by the antagonism we face from those who oppose you. We are also distressed when we endure seasons when your blessing seems absent. During these times encourage us to see the unchanging nature of your love, and remember your past blessings as the guarantee of your future blessing and help. In Jesus name. Amen.

Daily Reading Plan Day Three: Genesis 6–7; Psalm 3.

Day 4: *The Deepest Longing*

> *My soul is downcast within me; therefore I will remember you from the land of the Jordan, the heights of Hermon—from Mount Mizar. Deep calls to deep in the roar of your waterfalls; all your waves and breakers have swept over me. (Psalm 42:6–7)*

Our thirst for God comes from the depths of our souls. "Deep calls to deep"—the depths of our souls call out to the depths of God's heart. The billows and breakers—our sorrows and heart-breaking problems—uncover our souls and lay them bear (vv. 5, 11). One thing cannot change, however, for God is my God, the "God of my life." The deeper the sorrow, the deeper the joy will be, for through my sorrow God forms a deeper capacity in my life to receive from him. The process of sorrow, although painful, produces a quiet trust in God which, in an ongoing way, satisfies my thirst for him.

At times we may experience the heights of joy and blessing ("the heights of Hermon"), but at other times we pass through the deep valley of depression and painful experience ("the land of the Jordan"). These may be times when:

> *God does not show his face.*
>
> *The answer to our prayers does not come.*
>
> *Our soul is troubled and cast down.*

At these times, like the psalmist, we remember God. Far more importantly, he will remember us. He has promised "I will not forget you" (read Isaiah 49:15). God has already invested so much in us—the life of his only begotten Son—that he can never let us go.

> **Prayer:** Lord, thank you that when we pass though times of difficulty, you will not forget us. Your presence can be found even amid pain. Help us, Lord, to develop a quiet confidence in you, which will not be eroded in hard times. In Jesus name. Amen.

Daily Reading Plan Day Four: Genesis 8–9; Psalm 4.

Day 5: *A Determined Desire*

> *Why, my soul, are you downcast? Why so disturbed within me? Put your hope in God, for I will yet praise him, my Savior and my God. (Psalm 42:5, 11)*

Let's be honest. There are times when believers get depressed, or down in the dumps. Perhaps our picture of a Christian in victory is of someone brimming with joy and confidence, exuding faith to bless others. Yet the reality of our experience can be so different.

There are times when we are so discouraged, that we don't want to join in God's praises; we may avoid choosing happy or positive songs—a dirge seems more suitable to our mood!

Yet at these times, if we share the faith of the psalmist, we can choose to remember God (v. 6). These are times when our usual pattern of prayer may not work for us, and we must turn instead to pray to God honestly about our feelings (v. 9), and even express our doubts. We may not understand why bad things happen, but we can choose to trust and maintain our hope in God (v. 5, 11).

When the psalmist says, "I will yet praise him," this suggests that he had stopped praising him. It has been my experience that singing and praising God when I don't feel like it does my soul no end of good! This is no magic cure, no immediate answer, nor is it the result of some misplaced sense of duty toward God. Rather, it is the result of a sense of steady, deepening trust in the God whose ways are past finding out. After all, that was the way he led Israel in the desert—one step at a time. The pillar of fire and cloud which led them, also hid their destination from view.

> **Prayer:** Dear God, in times when we feel unable to praise you, strengthen our determination to do so. Grant that we may learn to trust when we cannot trace you, and praise you when we find little reason for joy. So let our desire for you become deeper, more settled, and not dependent on circumstances. Amen.

Daily Reading Plan Day Five: Genesis 9–10, Psalm 5.

Day 6: *More of What Tastes Good!*

> *Taste and see that the Lord is good; blessed is the one who takes refuge in him The lions may grow weak and hungry, but those who seek the Lord lack no good thing. (Psalm 34:8, 10)*

As we have seen, the basis for our desire for God is our past experience with him. We have already "tasted" and seen that the Lord is good, and so we are hungry for more. Indeed, the Bible compares the blessings God offers with a banquet, and the evangelist cries out: "Come, for everything is now ready" (Luke 14:17). God does not limit us to one taste, but wants us to receive from him repeatedly.

I am sure many readers will relate to my powerful, almost addictive, desire for chocolate! It's so nice! Whenever I taste it, I want more! (And of course, well-meaning friends keep buying it for me!) Yet, in the case of chocolate, it is possible to eat too much. We can make ourselves ill by over-indulgence (not to mention to put on weight)!

Thankfully, when it comes to God, I can take as much as I like, with no ill effects. The good effects I experience from my relationship with God keeps me coming back for more.

The Psalmist also describes what we might call the "nutritional value" of our experience with God. When we "taste and see that the Lord is good" we "lack no good thing." We will find in God all we need for spiritual life: strength to serve; patience to endure; love for the unlovely; hope for the future when all seems hopeless. The key to abundant blessing is our hunger and thirst for God—his goodness keeps us coming back for more!

> **Prayer:** Lord, we thank you that in Christ you have provided us with all we need for life and godliness. We recognise you as the source of all our blessings. We draw near to worship you for the blessings we have received, we open our hearts to receive from you again. In Jesus name. Amen.

Daily Reading Plan Day Six: Genesis 11–12; Psalm 6.

Day 7: God's *Constant Supply*

> *By day the Lord directs his love, at night his song is with me—a prayer to the God of my life. I say to God my Rock, "Why have you forgotten me? Why must I go about mourning, oppressed by the enemy?" My bones suffer mortal agony as my foes taunt me, saying to me all day long, "Where is your God?" (Psalm 42:8–10)*

Here is a strange mixture—so common in the Psalms—of honest prayer and faith in God. I find it strange because at the same time it acknowledges the psalmists view of his dire situation ("[God] why have you forgotten me?") and confesses God's love and song have never left him ("the Lord directs his love … his song is with me.")

We may face experiences where everything suggests that God has forgotten us. Yet deep inside we feel an assurance that this cannot be so. He has not forgotten us, and he will never abandon us. Deep within the believer's soul, the Holy Spirit gives this assurance. Jesus said that the Holy Spirit is like a well of living water within us, springing up to eternal life. If the oppression and taunting of the enemy ("where is your God?") and the physical suffering we experience ("my bones suffer mortal agony") represent the desert place of our experience, we can be sure that God will send us the strengthening, enabling water of his Spirit.

When Israel faced death by thirst in the wilderness, God instructed Moses to strike a rock, and water immediately gushed out. That Rock is Christ. He has already been struck for us, on the cross. His living water flows constantly to our soul in all circumstances. In the daytime, he directs his love, and in the darkest night, he gives us a song!

> **Prayer:** Lord, we thank you for your constant supply of love. We thank you that your Spirit assures us of your constant help in all circumstances. Help us to sing songs in the dark nights of our unpleasant experiences, that we may have a testimony to share with others, that "God is my Rock." Amen.

Daily Reading Plan Day Seven: Genesis 13–14; Psalm 7.

Psalm 63: My God, I Seek You

Day 8: *Seeking the Spring, not Broken Cisterns*

> *You, God, are my God, earnestly I seek you; I thirst for you, my whole being longs for you, in a dry and parched land where there is no water (Psalm 63:1)*

The beginning of Psalm 63 presents the psalmist's relationship with God: "you … are my God." This is a relationship shared by every Christian believer, and it creates within us an eagerness to seek God. Perhaps the psalmist's longing to be near God was encouraged by the words of the prophets (e.g. Jeremiah 29:13, "You will seek me and find me when you seek me with all your heart.") We should likewise be encouraged—God is longing to make himself known to us. After all, there would be no point in our seeking for God if he could not be found!

The psalmist's longing for God was so strong that it consumed his "whole being." Are we as eager as the psalmist to seek God? The parched, or desert, land which has no water speaks of the world around us—the world without Christ. The glories, joys and activities of the world ultimately fail to satisfy us. There is no water for the thirsty soul there. The saved man or woman can find no satisfaction except in God. Worldly pleasures are like the broken cisterns Jeremiah spoke of in Jer 213, "that cannot hold water." As an old hymn put it: "I tried the broken cisterns, Lord, But, ah, the waters failed; Even as I stooped to drink they fled, And mocked me as I wailed." We seek God, who is our "spring of living water." His waters, received as we seek him eagerly, cannot fail to satisfy.

> **Prayer:** Lord we thank you that, having tried the broken cisterns of this world, and found them worthless, we can turn to your Son and discover: "Now none but Christ can satisfy, None other name for me! There's love, and life, and lasting joy, Lord Jesus, found in Thee." In Jesus name. Amen.

Daily Reading Plan Day Eight: Genesis 15–16; Psalm 8.

Day 9: *Seeking God in the Sanctuary*

> *I have seen you in the sanctuary and beheld your power and your glory. (Psalm 63:2)*

We may question why the Psalms so frequently refer to God's people meeting with him "in the sanctuary," which is to say in the tabernacle, and later the temple. Certainly, God had ordained the tabernacle as a tent of meeting, a focal point of meeting between him and the people. God said to Moses:

> Then have them make a sanctuary for me, and I will dwell among them. (Exodus 25:8)

Yet Solomon, when dedicating the temple, recognised that: "The heavens, even the highest heaven, cannot contain [God]. How much less this temple I have built!" (1 Kings 8:27) As Jesus later affirmed, God can be worshipped anywhere (John 4:23).

So why did David think the place to find God was the tabernacle or sanctuary? Because he had received God's help there in the past. He had experienced something of God's power and glory, and so he wanted more.

O that all our churches could be places like this! It matters very little whether we consider our church buildings to be holy places, or just plain buildings where the body of Christ (the true church) meets. The important question is: why do people come to our church? It is to *encounter God in his power and glory*, and to be convinced, in the words of Saint Paul, that "God is really among you!" (1 Corinthians 14:25).

> **Prayer:** Lord, grant that our churches may be places for people to come and seek you; places where they might behold your power and your glory. Let them be convinced that Jesus Christ is alive because they can encounter the Living God dwelling among his people. In Jesus name. Amen.

Daily Reading Plan Day Nine: Genesis 17–18; Psalms 9.

Day 10: *Why Seek God?*

> *Because your love is better than life, my lips will glorify you. I will praise you as long as I live, and in your name I will lift up my hands. (Psalm 63:3–4)*

As Christians we gather to worship God in our local churches and home groups. Week after week, in all weathers, we spend time seeking God together in prayer and his word. Every day, many Christians can be found seeking God in private prayer time or (if the whole household are believers) in family devotions. But what is all this religious fervour about? It would quite reasonable for someone to ask us, "Why seek God?"

The psalmist gives us the answer in the above verses. Focussing on praise and worship, they reveal a deep inner motivation for praising God. The psalmist wants to sing ("my lips will glorify you"), and praise with his whole body ("I will lift up my hands"). He is determined never to stop praising God ("I will praise you as long as I live.")

So what is that motivation? The psalmist says, "your love is better than life." Having experienced God's love, the psalmist could find nothing else in his life experience which could compare with it. Some people put their whole life and soul into projects they believe in, hobbies that excite them, or jobs which they find reward them. We have found something much better than all these. No wonder we throw all our hearts into it! That is why we praise God, and the reason why we seek God—nothing can compare with the greatness of his love, demonstrated in what he has done for us in Jesus!

> **Prayer:** Dear God our Father, when we think of your love revealed in Jesus Christ our Lord, and his willingness to die in our place on the cross so that we might be forgiven, we are driven again and again to praise and glorify you. Because your love is better than all life can offer us, we worship you. Amen.

Daily Reading Plan Day Ten: Genesis 19–20; Psalm 10.

Day 11: *Full Satisfaction*

> *I will be fully satisfied as with the richest of foods; with singing lips my mouth will praise you. (Psalm 63:5)*

It is still a tragic reality that in the majority world, vast numbers of hungry people are unable to afford or obtain sufficient food. Many more are unable to obtain the kind of high-energy nutritious foods which truly satisfy their hunger. Whilst we do all we can to alleviate the poverty and hunger of our fellow men and women, we must understand that the psalmist is using his description of "the richest foods" which deeply satisfied his hunger as a metaphor for the blessings of God.

God has not called us to seek him in vain. There is no need for any of us to be hungry in the sense of our spiritual needs. God has provided the rich food of his word: "When your words came, I ate them; they were my joy and my heart's delight, for I bear your name, Lord God Almighty." (Jer 15:16)

More than this, God has given us true bread to eat. Jesus said, "For the bread of God is the bread that comes down from heaven and gives life to the world … I am the bread of life. Whoever comes to me will never go hungry, and whoever believes in me will never be thirsty."

Our hunger for God—and the blessings of love, joy, and peace he brings—can be satisfied as we begin and continue our relationship with his Son Jesus Christ. The book of Revelation describes the consummation of that relationship, in our heavenly home, with these words: "Never again will they hunger; never again will they thirst." Because of this, we will begin right now to sing and praise him with joyful lips!

> **Prayer:** Lord, we thank you for your written word, the Scriptures, which present to us your living word, Jesus Christ your Son. We praise you with joyful lips, because our relationship with you, through Christ, deeply satisfies our souls now, and will satisfy us forever. In Jesus name. Amen.

Daily Reading Plan Day Eleven: Genesis 21–22; Psalm 11.

Day 12: *Longing for God on our Beds*

> *On my bed I remember you; I think of you through the watches of the night. Because you are my help, I sing in the shadow of your wings. (Psalm 63:6–7)*

Watching a movie, reading a good book, listening to an interesting radio broadcast. These are all ways in which people may choose to relax in bed before turning off the light and going to sleep. We can be sure the psalmist did not have had access to any of these things—and yet perhaps his suggestion is the best one of all.

Our longing for God does not end when we close our Bible reading notes, come home from church, or even when we retire to bed. At night, the psalmist remembered God: he meditated on his word and his works; he recalled his help; he felt safe, as a chick beneath its mother's wings; and he rejoiced. The best thing to take to bed with you is a desire for God, and a constant experience of his presence in which we find fulness of joy.

> *How priceless is your unfailing love, O God! People take refuge in the shadow of your wings. They feast on the abundance of your house; you give them drink from your river of delights. (Psalm 36:7–8)*

> *You make known to me the path of life; you will fill me with joy in your presence, with eternal pleasures at your right hand. (Psalm 16:11)*

In our stressful modern lifestyles, when various remedies are available to help us relax and sleep, perhaps the best of them is still the sense of joy, peace, and satisfaction in our hearts as we rest "in the shadow if his wings."

> **Prayer:** Dear God, from the beginning of our day, until we go to sleep at night, help us to remember you. Help us to think of you in the watches of the night. Bless us with your peace and rest, as we find security, "in the shadow of your wings." In Jesus name. Amen.

Daily Reading Plan Day Twelve: Genesis 23–24; Psalm 12.

Day 13: *Drawn to Desire God by His Grace*

I cling to you; your right hand upholds me (Psalm 63:8)

This is the basic principle of biblical spirituality. All true spiritual progress is based on a desire for God. We go on with God in direct proportion to our desire for him, and so the psalmist says, "I cling to you," or as the AV translates it "My soul followeth hard after thee."

Yet notice that grace is the source of our desire, and its cause. For even as I seek after God, it is God who draws me to himself, and his right hand that upholds me in that effort—his grace breeds my desire. This may be what John means when he writes:

Out of his fullness we have all received grace in place of grace already given. (John 1:16)

The more we receive by God's grace, the more we desire; and so the more we receive! Similarly, the more we experience in our relationship with God, the more we appreciate that we need him.

These two ideas—our desire for God and his drawing us to himself by grace—are not in opposition. Rather, they are to work in cooperation. And so, whilst the Scripture affirms that entry into the kingdom is a gift of grace, Jesus also exhorts his hearers:

Make every effort to enter through the narrow door (Luke 13:24)

Receiving grace makes us hungry and thirsty for God. It never makes us indifferent or lazy in the pursuit of his kingdom!

> **Prayer:** Lord, the way in which you have drawn us to yourself through grace makes us hungry and thirsty for more of you. Grant your right hand of strength will support us as we make it our aim to seek you and know you more. In Jesus name. Amen.

Daily Reading Plan Day Thirteen: Genesis 25–26; Psalm 13.

Day 14: *God will Protect His Seeking People*

> *Those who want to kill me will be destroyed; they will go down to the depths of the earth. They will be given over to the sword and become food for jackals. But the king will rejoice in God; all who swear by God will glory in him, while the mouths of liars will be silenced. (Psalm 63:9–11)*

It is a sobering thought that the psalmist (in this case David) sought God, and wrote these inspired prayers, whilst his life was being hunted down by jealous enemies (see the full story of how king Saul, jealous of David's rise to prominence, sought to kill him, in 1 Samuel 18–31 A similar situation arose when Davis's ambitious son Absalom sought his life in 2 Samuel 14–18). All of Psalm 63 can be seen in the light of such a background. It seems that the more trouble David was in, the more he sought God. He longed to take refuge in the God whom he called "my refuge and my fortress" (see Psalm 18:2).

What is our reaction to times of testing? We may not be facing the difficulties which David faced — people trying to kill us — but we will still face a range of distressing experiences. Bereavement, family conflict or misunderstanding, painful or even terminal illness. If we learn from the psalmist's example, then rather than blame God for these situations, we will lift our hearts in prayer with more desire for God than ever.

As a result of this attitude, according to verse 11, we shall rejoice. The terrible circumstances David faced never finally overwhelmed him. Turning to God did not mean he was running from reality. His refuge and fortress were not make-believe. Instead he proved God to be "an ever-present help in trouble" (Psalm 46:1).

> **Prayer:** O Lord our God, we thank you that in the distressing experiences of life, we have proved you to be "an ever-present help." Lord, as we set our hearts to seek you despite trying circumstances, may we find the strength to rejoice. In Jesus name. Amen.

Daily Reading Plan Day Fourteen: Genesis 27–28; Psalm 14.

Psalm 84: My God, I Long for Your Courts
Day 15: *"There am I With Them"*

> *How lovely is your dwelling place, Lord Almighty! My soul yearns, even faints, for the courts of the Lord; my heart and my flesh cry out for the living God. (Psalm 84:1–2)*

I wonder if any church ministers reading these words have experienced long queues of people, eagerly waiting outside their church on a Sunday morning, desperate for worship to begin?! I have, in fact, witnessed such things, but admittedly, never in the UK, and never when I've been the preacher! As a teenager I once lined up outside an auditorium in downtown Los Angeles, with 8,000 other believers waiting to hear a prominent Christian speaker. The worship and singing started long before the doors opened, and I still recall the wonderful presence of God.

The reason the psalmist—and many other pilgrims—were so eager to travel up to Jerusalem, to worship in the temple of God was a profoundly simple one. They felt God's presence there. They experienced "God with us." For them, the regular pilgrimage to the holy festivals kept them in touch, not only with the religious tradition handed down by their ancestors, but with the Living God.

Today, the idea of a "house of God" or a "sacred space" is frowned on by many in the Christian community, who rightly see the church as the body of believers. It's about people not buildings! Yet whilst church meeting places *are* only buildings, what we come together to do in them is special, unique, and sacred. Jesus promised, "For where two or three gather in my name, there am I with them" (Matthew 18:20). If we are crying out with all our being for the living God, then the we must begin to seek him together with our Christian brothers and sisters. Where two or three are, we'll find Jesus there.

> **Prayer:** Dear God, grant that our churches may be places where, as we come together in your name, we will find you in our midst. In Jesus name. Amen.

Daily Reading Plan Day Fifteen: Genesis 29–30; Psalm 15.

Day 16: *I Long to be Near You, My King and My God*

> *Even the sparrow has found a home, and the swallow a nest for herself, where she may have her young—a place near your altar, Lord Almighty, my King and my God. (Psalm 84:3)*

How the psalmist longed to stay in God's presence, in the holy place of the temple, that he might be nearer to God. There is no doubt that the desire to be near to God is a good one, and has been expressed in a myriad of ways by Christians through the years. Think of the hymn by Sarah Adams, "Nearer my God to Thee," which was reportedly played by the string ensemble aboard the Titanic as the ship sank. Or what about William Cowper's "O For a Closer Walk with God" and countless other hymns and worship songs right up to the present day. Do songs like these express the desire of your heart to be closer to the heart of God?

In Psalm 84, it seems that the psalmist was jealous of the sparrows and swallows. These birds, he could see, had found a home in the temple. They never needed to leave to return to the pressing business or life. Oh, that he could be like them, and remain always at worship!

We cannot spend all our time in worship, or in a place of worship. We must go out into the world with its business and responsibilities. And yet as we do, we will find God with us there—he promises to be *near us*. Jesus said:

> *Are not two sparrows sold for a penny? Yet not one of them will fall to the ground outside your Father's care. And even the very hairs of your head are all numbered. So don't be afraid; you are worth more than many sparrows. (Matthew 10:29–31)*

> **Prayer:** Lord, we cannot always be occupied with the blessed task of worshipping you, gathered together in your name. But just as in nature you allow birds to be near your altar, so you assure your people, who are "worth more than many sparrows," of your constant presence. Praise God! Amen

Daily Reading Plan Day Sixteen: Genesis 31–32; Psalm 16.

Day 17: *I Just Can't Wait to Praise You Again!*

> *Blessed are those who dwell in your house; they are ever praising you. (Psalm 84:4)*

In yesterday's reading, we saw how God would be *near us* even when we cannot be *near him* (which, as the psalmist saw it, meant worshipping in the temple). Today's verse follows on from there. For although we cannot always be "in your house," "ever praising you," the psalmist's language indicates the high regard in which he held every opportunity to set time aside and go along to worship. He is basically saying "I can't wait to get back to God's house and worship you again! My praise there is a pledge of my praise never ending praise to God!"

True, we may live in a different age, and a different dispensation, but none of that really matters in this instance—for the desire we have for God should be the same throughout all time. Our longing to worship, praise, and glorify our God should be as strong as the psalmist's. We too should consider those "blessed" who are able to gather for worship, and long intensely to be among them.

I have now been in pastoral ministry for nearly 30 years. During that time, I have experienced seasons when going to church was difficult. The same place, the same songs, the same people, every week. It can lead to staleness in our Christian experience. What is the answer? Changing the service, learning the latest worship songs, inviting fresh speakers or other Christian groups to join us can all help. But fundamentally, what we need when we are spiritually stale is A NEW ATTITUDE. Let's be refreshed in our longing and desire to be "ever praising you!"

> **Prayer:** Lord, how blessed are those who dwell in your house, they are forever praising you. How grateful we are, that we can be among them. E praise you for the great day when heaven will open, and we will praise you around your throne forever. In Jesus name. Amen.

Daily Reading Plan Day Seventeen: Genesis 33–34; Psalm 17.

Day 18: *Finding Joy in Tribulation*

> *Blessed are those whose strength is in you, whose hearts are set on pilgrimage. As they pass through the Valley of Baka, they make it a place of springs; the autumn rains also cover it with pools. (Psalm 84:5–6)*

It is one thing for our desire toward God to be evident when we are filled with joy, or gathered with a group of other believers in worship. But the psalmist's thought here takes a different turn. What about those who are passing through the Valley of Baka? (Baka means "trouble") Christians who pass through tribulation can choose to do two things: 1) find their strength in God; and 2) set their hearts on pilgrimage.

We sometimes face experiences for which we lack the strength to cope. At these times we must find our strength in God alone; then we will be the kind of people who, when we pass through the valley of tears, turn it into joy, "a place of springs." No matter what this world may throw at us, we are not staying here forever. Our troubles are only for a time. Every believer is a pilgrim, travelling through this world, on our way to heaven, for *"our citizenship is in heaven. And we eagerly await a Savior from there, the Lord Jesus Christ"* (Philippians 3:20).

After facing trials and tribulations which he described as "beyond our ability to endure," Saint Paul wrote to encourage others facing similar difficulties:

> *Therefore we do not lose heart. Though outwardly we are wasting away, yet inwardly we are being renewed day by day. For our light and momentary troubles are achieving for us an eternal glory that far outweighs them all. So we fix our eyes not on what is seen, but on what is unseen, since what is seen is temporary, but what is unseen is eternal. (2 Corinthians 4:16–18)*

> **Prayer:** Lord, I admit that sometimes I find life difficult. Grant that your joy and strength shall spring up to comfort and console me. Let me share what you have given me with others. In Jesus name. Amen

Daily Reading Plan Day Eighteen: Genesis 35–36; Psalm 18.

Day 19: *Strength for Every Day*

> *They go from strength to strength, till each appears before God in Zion. (Psalm 84:7)*

The strength we receive from God during trouble is not a one-off or a passing thing. Having proved God to be sufficient in one difficult circumstance, we learn to trust him in other situations, relying solely on his strength not ours, so that we are able to cope with more of the troubles which life throws at us with serenity—not resignation, but with the calm certainty of God's ultimate victory. Through Jesus, we will have the strength to cope with life's trials.

By nature, when human beings grow older, they become weaker, not stronger. But with Jesus, there is a strength which grows in our experience every day: a strength of faith, desire, and expectation for the coming of the time when we shall "appear before God in Zion." This is the blessed hope of every believer. We are waiting "for the blessed hope—the appearing of the glory of our great God and Savior, Jesus Christ" (Titus 2:13). From that time on, "we will be with the Lord forever" (1 Thessalonians 4:17).

Jesus repeatedly spoke to his disciples about the time when he would come again, and receive them to himself (see John 14:3). He told them to remain in a state of readiness, watching, praying, and serving (e.g. Matthew 25:13; Mark 13:33; Luke 21:36). As we make it our aim to do this, we can be sure that his never-failing supply of strength will be all we need.

> **Prayer: Lord, w**e thank you, for the strength you give us day by day, that we might be faithful to you in all that we do. We do not know when you will come again, but we know that you are able to keep us watching, praying, and serving until that wonderful day when we are "forever with the Lord." Amen.

Daily Reading Plan Day Eighteen: Genesis 37–38; Psalm 19.

Day 20: *My Longing for God's House*

> *Hear my prayer, Lord God Almighty; listen to me, God of Jacob. Look on our shield, O God; look with favor on your anointed one. Better is one day in your courts than a thousand elsewhere; I would rather be a doorkeeper in the house of my God than dwell in the tents of the wicked. (Psalm 84:8–10)*

The psalmist is here praying for God's mercy upon the nation as well as for himself. His prayer is that God would look upon the King of Israel ("your anointed one") with favour. In some way, he links this with his own ability to attend temple worship. Certainly, there was a need for national stability if the worship of the nation was to continue. Throughout Israel's history, when the king turned away from God, most of the nation inevitably followed, and the temple and the worship of Yahweh were neglected.

For the psalmist, the temple was not only the centre of national worship, it was the centre of his own life too. According to the inscription, the psalmist was "of the sons of Korah", who were appointed as doorkeepers in the temple (1 Chronicles 9:19). Yet whilst the doorkeeper's role may be understood as a lowly service, the psalmist would prefer the lowest place than to dwell among the wicked and be excluded from worship of God.

Is our desire for God as great as that of the psalmist? Would we prefer a place as a doorkeeper in God's house to dwelling in the ease of wealth and, luxury? Would we prefer one day in God's presence than a thousand elsewhere?

> **Prayer:** Dear Lord, we pray for our nation, that all people might be free to attend the worship of God without restriction, and that our God may be held in high esteem by all people. We would rather spend one day worshipping you, than a thousand elsewhere. In Jesus name. Amen.

Daily Reading Plan Day Nineteen: Genesis 39–40; Psalm 20.

Day 21: *God who Satisfies my Soul*

> *For the Lord God is a sun and shield; the Lord bestows favor and honor; no good thing does he withhold from those whose walk is blameless. Lord Almighty, blessed is the one who trusts in you. (Psalm 84:11–12)*

We cannot tell others of God's wonderful salvation until we have experienced it for ourselves. This is the message of the verse above us. As Isaiah declared the salvation of God to others, he did so from personal experience: 'God is my salvation … my defence'.

It is reassuring that as we set out to worship and serve God throughout the Christmas season, his plan is that we should have a personal encounter with him, so that we might share the blessings which we receive from that encounter with others.

When the shepherds came to Bethlehem, in response to the message of the angel, they encountered Christ for themselves. They told Mary and Joseph about what the angel had said, and as they left the scene, and probably for many days afterward, they told everyone they met about the remarkable events of that first Christmas night.

Having once encountered God as our Saviour, we are motivated to share him with others. Church evangelism is not a cynical or narrow-minded programme which exists solely that we may convert others to our own point of view. Rather, it is the activity of a once hungry, but now satisfied soul, who wants to share what he/she has received with others. When I lived in Cardiff, I befriended a group of homeless people. If a meal was on offer at the Salvation Army soup kitchen, or a bed for the night was free at the shelter, they were always keen to tell other homeless people about it, and pass on the good news.

Having experienced so much from God, let's not be mean! Pass it on!

> **Prayer:** God my Saviour, as you have blessed my life with your strength hand deliverance, help me to bless others by telling them how they too may know you as their salvation. In Jesus name. Amen.

Daily Reading Plan Day Twenty: Genesis 41; Psalm 21.

Selected Psalms: My God, I Seek Your Face

Day 22: *Thirsting in a Parched Land*

Lord, hear my prayer, listen to my cry for mercy; in your faithfulness and righteousness come to my relief. Do not bring your servant into judgment, for no one living is righteous before you. The enemy pursues me, he crushes me to the ground; he makes me dwell in the darkness like those long dead. So my spirit grows faint within me; my heart within me is dismayed. I remember the days of long ago; I meditate on all your works and consider what your hands have done. I spread out my hands to you; I thirst for you like a parched land. (Psalm 143:1–6)

Psalm 143 presents another aspect of thirsting for God. Having experienced overwhelming opposition from his enemies, David compares himself with a land that has had no rain for a long time. Famine conditions were prevailing in his heart, the pasture and vegetation were gone. Sometimes, tough experiences can leave us feeling without the graces of our faith, desperately in need of fresh blessing. What a parched land needs is rain, and what the struggling believer needs is the filling of the Holy Spirit. In times of famine, neither too much nor too little rain is needed. Similarly, the believer needs a constant, dependable supply of grace. When David felt barren, he longed for showers of blessing and stretched out his hands in prayer to wait for God.

Isaiah describes God's Word as refreshing rain that goes out from him to water the earth. It brings blessings and produces praise (see Isaiah 52:10–12). It accomplished God's will for our lives. God may take us through may dry times, but they are never truly barren times if they produce in us a deeper sense of trust, and a more constant longing and desire for our God.

Prayer: Lord, we confess that, sometimes, we feel dry and our lives are barren. Send the water of your Spirit to refill our lives, and the water of your word to make us fruitful again. Amen.

Daily Reading Plan Day One: Genesis 42; Psalm 22.

Day 23: *The Abundance of God's House*

> *How priceless is your unfailing love, O God! People take refuge in the shadow of your wings. They feast on the abundance of your house; you give them drink from your river of delights. For with you is the fountain of life; in your light we see light. (Psalm 36:7–9)*

Our hunger and thirst for God shall be generously rewarded, for as we take refuge in the shadow of his wings, we discover the abundance he provides. The psalmist describes this abundance as like that of a feast, one provided by a great king. Unlike the feast of earthly kings, however, the drink on offer is not wine (e.g. Esther 1:7). The drink God provides for our souls flows like a river containing the purest water.

In his vision of heaven, the apostle John saw a pure river of the water of life (Rev 22:1 – a symbol of the Holy Spirit), proceeding from the throne of God and flowing to the city (Rev 22:2 – which is itself a picture of the church). The drink we receive at God's feast therefore comes direct from his throne to our hearts. We are invited to come to the water and drink (Isa 55:1; Rev 22:17), and the abundance of blessing God offers is truly breath-taking.

I live in a part of South Wales which contains one of the fastest flowing rivers in the British Isles. As teenagers we found it ideal for white-water canoeing! Yet at its broadest it is only a few metres wide. Flying once over Canada, my eyes were opened by the vast width of the rivers beneath us. "That's what God's river must be like!" I thought to myself. What is more, God's river is never stale, for the psalmist also calls it a fountain. When Ezekiel saw this same river he declared "Where the river flows, everything will live" (Ezek 47:9). Thank God, as we seek him, we will not merely exist—we shall truly *live* in his light!

> **Prayer:** Lord, we praise you for the abundance of your supply. You are pleased to give your Spirit and the blessings of your kingdom to all who seek and ask. Grant that today we shall be satisfied in you as we live in your light. In Jesus name. Amen.

Daily Reading Plan Day One: Genesis 43; Psalm 23.

Day 24: *The Only Thing I Desire*

> *One thing I ask from the Lord, this only do I seek: that I may dwell in the house of the Lord all the days of my life, to gaze on the beauty of the Lord and to seek him in his temple. (Psalm 27:4)*

The psalmist may have encountered many blessings in life, but none of these compared with the experience he had enjoyed when God revealed himself during temple worship and the reading of the Scriptures. God had been present in his time of worship. He had encountered God in such a way that he no longer desired anything else "one thing I ask from the Lord, this only do I seek."

As Christians, we too have experienced a "meeting" with God, for we have believed in his Son, Jesus Christ. It is no longer through the temple worship or the writings of the prophets alone that God reveals himself, for he has, "in these last days spoke to us by his son." (Hebrews 1:2) Jesus not only brings us God's word but directly displays his nature and beauty to us, for:

> *The Son is the radiance of God's glory and the exact representation of his being, (Hebrews 1:3a)*

Having seen "God's glory displayed in the face of Jesus Christ" (2 Corinthians 4:6) we lose our desire for lesser things; we no longer pursue our worldly interests with such attention. Our eyes and hearts are fixed on higher things. Our hunger thirst and passion for God can become all consuming. But, according to the psalmist, this is not a bad thing. Rather, it is the "one thing" that really matters.

> **Prayer:** Father God, having already experienced life and blessing through faith in your son Jesus Christ, we long for more of you. Our hearts' desire is to see your glory and beauty in the face of Jesus, as you daily reveal yourself to us. This is the "one thing" we will seek above all others today. In Jesus name. Amen.

Daily Reading Plan Day One: Genesis 44; Psalm 24.

Day 25: *Are You Selfish or Selfless?*

> *Take delight in the Lord, and he will give you the desires of your heart. (Psalm 37:4)*

A promise like this immediately grabs my attention. Is God promising me anything I desire? Does the psalmist really suppose that the Creator can be compared with the Aladdin's genie, who would grant three wishes to whoever rubbed the magic lamp? Actually, no; but a closer look at the psalm brings out that God's promise involves something far greater than readers of the Arabian fairy tale could imagine!

The promise that God will "give you the desires of your heart" is given to those who "take delight in the Lord." When our hearts are fixed on the things of God, our desires will be such that an infinitely wise God shall be able to grant them, for they will accord with his will. The things we must desire, according to Paul, are things above:

> *Since, then, you have been raised with Christ, set your hearts on things above, where Christ is, seated at the right hand of God. Set your minds on things above, not on earthly things. (Colossians 3:1–2)*

When we desire the things that come from God, he will give us the desires of our heart; for example: the Holy Spirit (Luke 11:13); divine wisdom (James 1:5); understanding to know and do his will (Colossians 1:9; 1 John 5:14). When we indulge in selfish desire, we will receive no answer.

> *When you ask, you do not receive, because you ask with wrong motives, that you may spend what you get on your pleasures. (James 4:3)*

But today, I take delight in the Lord. I desire him more than anything else, and so, I can take the sweetness of this promise. It cannot fail: "he will give you the desires of your heart."

> **Prayer:** Lord, today and always, let our hearts be in tune with your will, so that you may give us the desires of our hearts. In Jesus name. Amen.

Daily Reading Plan Day One: Genesis 45; Psalm 25.

Day 26: *My Only Desire*

> *Whom have I in heaven but you? And earth has nothing I desire besides you. My flesh and my heart may fail, but God is the strength of my heart and my portion forever. (Psalm 73:25–26)*

In Psalm 73 as a whole, the psalmist has expressed disappointment in his life, which had not lived up to his expectations (73:13–14). He was especially distressed when he saw the success of the wicked, and the comparative lack of ease and prosperity endured by the godly (73:2–5). He even admitted to moaning like an animal and complaining to God about this lot (73:21–22).

But when the truth occurred to him, as he sat in the sanctuary of God, that when viewed from eternity rather than time, the lot of the righteous was vastly superior to that of the wicked, he began to count his blessings and his hope was renewed.

In fact, the psalmist's eyes were turned towards God in heaven. This is the ultimate answer to the problems we experience of life. By focussing on our relationship with God, we get a fresh viewpoint. No matter what this world might throw at us—injustice, poverty, prejudice—we are guaranteed God's continual presence (73:23a), kept by his unfailing love (73:23b), continually guided by his infinite wisdom (73:24a), and assured of our eternal home with God in heaven (73:24b).

Ultimately, God is our source and our goal. He is the reason we can go through life with endurance and faith, and he is the reward at the end of our journey.

> **Prayer:** Lord, we praise you for the assurance of your abiding presence now, your wise guidance through life, and the promise of our eternal life with you. Grant that when we face the disappointments and discouragement of life, that we may find hope in your unfailing love. In Jesus name. Amen.

Daily Reading Plan Day One: Genesis 46; Psalm 26.

Day 27: *Longing for God's Commands*

> *I open my mouth and pant, longing for your commands. (Psalm 119:131)*

So far in this devotional, through a selection of scriptures taken from the Psalms, we have contemplated the theme of longing and thirsting for God. Today's verse presents us with a somewhat different, although related, theme. The psalmist here expresses his longing for God's commandments.

By nature, human beings tend to resent commandments—no one likes being told what to do. A lifetime of being forced to do something we would not chose of our own volition is slavery. Clearly, the psalmist did not see obedience to God in these terms. For him, the blessing and joy of doing God's commands led him to long for them. For the believer, loving God means we take delight in obeying his commands.

When Jesus was about to leave his disciples, he introduced them to the principle of love expressed as obedience. Jesus said:

> "If you love me, keep my commands. … Whoever has my commands and keeps them is the one who loves me. The one who loves me will be loved by my Father, and I too will love them and show myself to them." (John 14:15, 21)

Therefore, obeying God is no burden for the believer. Moreover, as the psalmist knew, "in obeying [God's commands/laws] there is great reward" (Psalm 19:11). The desire to please and obey God is as basic to the Christian life as the desire for air or water. That is why we open our mouths and pant for his commands.

> **Prayer:** Lord, we love you because you first loved us. Our longing and desire is to love you, and loving you means to obey your commands. Teach us to walk in your ways, and do your will, for our highest pleasure is to please you. In Jesus name. Amen.

Daily Reading Plan Day One: Genesis 47; Psalm 27.

Day 28: *Satisfaction for Our Hunger and Thirst*

> *Let them give thanks to the Lord for his unfailing love and his wonderful deeds for mankind, for he satisfies the thirsty and fills the hungry with good things. (Psalm 107:8–9)*

In this psalm, God is praised repeatedly for his "unfailing love and his wonderful deeds for mankind" (vv. 8, 15, 21, 31). This refrain is set against the background of God redeeming Israel from slavery in Egypt. Hungry and thirsty in the desert, they cried out to God, and he answered by providing water for them to drink and manna to eat (vv. 1–7).

> *He led you through the vast and dreadful wilderness, that thirsty and waterless land, with its venomous snakes and scorpions. He brought you water out of hard rock. He gave you manna to eat in the wilderness, something your ancestors had never known, to humble and test you so that in the end it might go well with you. (Deuteronomy 8:15–16)*

The apostle Paul saw God's goodness to Israel as an object lesson to prove God's love for all believers. Just as God satisfied Israel's physical thirst in the desert, so he satisfies our spiritual thirst today:

> *They all ate the same spiritual food and drank the same spiritual drink; for they drank from the spiritual rock that accompanied them, and that rock was Christ. (1 Corinthians 10:3–4)*

There can be many reasons why our souls feel hunger, or painful longing. A lack of love in one's life can lead to a great kind of hunger. Loneliness is the expression of our deep hunger for fellowship with other human beings. Ambition could be defined as the hunger to better ourselves, or improve our status. Like the psalmist, Paul had learned a vital spiritual secret: all these longings, every thirst the human soul may ever experience, can be satisfied by God.

> **Prayer:** Lord, we pray for all who are experiencing the spiritual hunger of loss, loneliness or pain. Grant that you will visit and save them, providing in your own mysterious way, that they may be *satisfied*, and *filled with good things*. Amen.

Daily Reading Plan Day One: Genesis 48; Psalm 28.

Day 29: *Desire Fulfilled*

> *The Lord is near to all who call on him, to all who call on him in truth. He fulfills the desires of those who fear him; he hears their cry and saves them. (Psalm 145:18–19)*

Following on from yesterday's reading, the psalmist highlights the way in which God saves his people from distress and "fulfills the desires of those who fear him." The psalm further defines for us "those who fear him" as those who "call on him" in prayer, and who "love him" (v. 20). I trust that includes everyone reading these notes right now! If so, you can be sure he is near you, and that he will respond to your cry for help.

The context of the psalm provides us with clues about the response we can expect from God. If the present generation is to tell the next generation "of [God's] mighty acts" (v. 4), then we must expect God to be at work in our lives. If we are to "speak of [God's] might" (v. 11), then we ought to be able to observe God's power everyday in creation, and in his sovereign rule over humanity (v. 11). Most of all, we should expect to experience God's nearness at difficult times:

> *The Lord upholds all who fall and lifts up all who are bowed down. (Psalm 145:14)*

Our personal, private desires, may be somewhat small when compared with the greatness of the world which God must govern. But we are never beneath his notice. God is great (v. 3) but he is also gracious and compassionate (v. 8), righteous in all his ways and faithful in all he does (v. 17). We can be sure that today he will direct as much of his attention and time to his children's personal needs as he gives to his vast creation!

> **Prayer:** Lord, we praise that such is your greatness, you are able to attend to great and small matters alike. You keep the vast universe in space, and perform mighty deeds, and yet you are near us when we cry out to you in distress, to help us and fulfil our desires. We give you thanks in Jesus name. Amen.

Daily Reading Plan Day One: Genesis 49; Psalm 29.

Day 30: *The Lord is Great!*

> *But may all who seek you rejoice and be glad in you; may those who long for your saving help always say, "The Lord is great! (Psalm 40:16)*

The psalms frequently repeat the refrain "Great is the Lord, and greatly to be praised" (see Psalm 48:1; 96:4; 145:3). God's greatness is praised for a wide variety of reasons. In Psalm 48, God is great and greatly to be praised because he had rescued Jerusalem from an invasion of an enemy king (see especially v. 4). In Psalm 96, God is great and to be praised because he is the creator. In Psalm 145 he is great and to be praised because of his mighty acts performed on behalf of his people from generation to generation.

Here in Psalm 40, "The Lord is great!" is the exclamation of someone who has called on God in their distress and experienced his saving help. The psalm begins:

> *I waited patiently for the Lord; he turned to me and heard my cry. He lifted me out of the slimy pit, out of the mud and mire; he set my feet on a rock and gave me a firm place to stand. He put a new song in my mouth, a hymn of praise to our God. Many will see and fear the Lord and put their trust in him. (Psalm 40:1–3)*

Never feel ashamed to pray and call on God in times of sorrow or distress. God does not sit in heaven and say, "there you are, you only ever come to me when you have a problem!" Rather, when we seek God is our distress, he will make us "rejoice and be glad" in him. He will certainly act on our behalf, and when he does, this will give us great cause to say continually, "the Lord is great!"

> **Prayer:** Lord, we thank you for the many times when you have answered our call of distress. In sorrow and bereavement, in sickness and fear of the future, in financial difficulty and worry over debt, through misunderstandings and strained relations with family and church members, your answers have repeatedly caused us to stand up and say, "the Lord is great!" Amen.

Daily Reading Plan Day One: Genesis 50; Psalm 30.

www.ingramcontent.com/pod-product-compliance
Lightning Source LLC
Chambersburg PA
CBHW061316040426
42444CB00010B/2665